Is God Nice?

By David Nagai

Illustrated by
Victoria Adhikari

For my neighbors in the slums who taught
me about God's love and beauty.

-David

For Roi – you inspire me to bring change
and courage to your generation. May you
and your friends bring more light, love and
peace to this world!

-Victoria

Note to Parents

I hope that each parent/reader can use this book as a jumping off point for thinking critically about how we view God and how that impacts the way we live in our world. May this book help you in your very important role of raising kids to be compassionate and courageous.

Where there is vagueness, I hope you can take the liberty to add details that suit your child.

Where concrete images don't work for you or may cause confusion for your child, please ignore it and focus on what does work.

I truly hope that this book can ignite questions, conversations and ongoing imagination. When your child suprises you with questions and ideas, remember that they are also our teachers. Divine wisdom is everywhere, if only we are humbly open.

Enjoy the book!
David Nagai

What is God like?

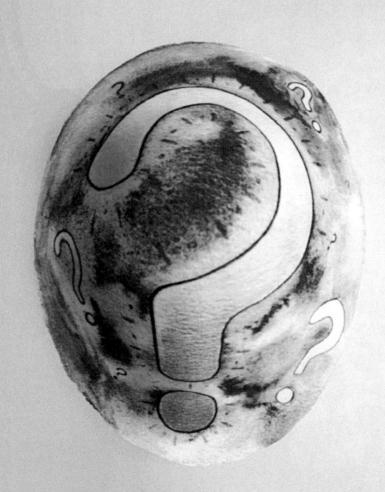

Is God nice?

God is more
wonderful than we
can ever fully imagine.

Let's take a look at
what God is like.

God is like a caring grandma.

She always wants you to sit
on her lap and hear about
your day. She wants to listen
to everything you have to say.

God loves listening to your
stories, ideas and questions.

God is like a kid at school
who stands up to a bully.

Sometimes he calls for
help or shows them a way
to escape. But sometimes
he can only stand there
and suffer with them.

When kids get bullied,
God is with them and
feels their pain.

God is like a doctor.

She cares for us when we're hurt or sick and helps us get better.

It might take time and feel uncomfortable, but God wants to heal us.

God is like a boy at recess who invites his friend in a wheelchair to join the game.

He cares more about including people than about winning or about what people think.

God shows us that real winners include all people.

God is like a kid at school who's kind to kids no matter how they look. Big, small, or different – it doesn't matter!

When other kids make fun of them, she says to stop being mean! She also says nice things about them and calls them her friends. Even if kids start making fun of her for it, she doesn't care, because she's brave and strong.

God stands up for people who get picked on.

God is like a judge who has to decide how to punish a mean man who did many horrible things.

The judge knows that this man needs love and compassion more than anything.

So, the judge decides not to put the man in jail forever. Instead, he invites him to live with his family and become his son.

God always forgives us and includes us as family no matter what we've done!

God is like a kid at school who invites everyone to sit with him at lunchtime.

When he welcomes kids who might feel different and not fit in, they know they're important and valuable, just the way they are!

God includes everyone at the lunch table.

God is like a gardener who recycles guns into shovels.

Instead of using guns to hurt people, she turns them into shovels to plant beautiful flowers and tasty veggies.

God wants to
change hurtful things
into beautiful and loving things.

God is like a girl who makes friends with people who have different color skin from her.

She doesn't like it when people are separated into groups because of their skin color. When she is with these new friends, everyone sees how beautiful and fun it is.

God wants to get to know all types of people!

God is like a kid
who helps refugees.

Refugees come from a country that's
so scary and dangerous that they run
away to find a safe place to live.

God always welcomes people
who need a place to live, no
matter where they're from.

God is like a kid at school
who hangs out with a kid
who has no friends.

Other kids don't like him
because his clothes are old
and dirty, and he sometimes
smells bad. But God doesn't
mind what people wear or
what they smell like.

God hangs out with all people
and isn't afraid of becoming
smelly or dirty.

God is like a boy who sees a big
kid hitting a little kid.

He steps between them and
starts doing the silliest dance
you can imagine! Then he
starts making animal noises
until everyone stops to watch!

God does wild things to help
people think about their actions
and so they stop hurting others.

God is like a kid who tattles on an adult for doing something bad to another kid. She makes sure that nobody – teachers, parents, or anyone – hurts kids!

God calls out hurtful actions so that kids can feel safe and respected.

God is like a teddy bear.
When you're afraid or
lonely, it helps you calm
down and sleep.

God is always with us
when we feel afraid or
lonely.

God is like a mom who lifts a
car off of her son's crushed leg.

God uses power to love and
care for people in need.

God is like a boy who's kind to mean bullies.

Sometimes he shares his candy with them,
invites them to play, or says kind words to
them. He knows that bullies are often mean
because they feel weak, afraid and lonely.
That's why they need special love so that
they can become strong enough to be nice.

God is like a man who sees a person without a home and asks him his name.

Then he invites the man to eat lunch with him at a nearby restaurant.

God wants to listen to people's stories and to be their friend.

God is so big and
mysterious that we can
never fully understand
what God is like.

God is not just a woman or
just a man. But, a long time
ago, someone came into the
world and showed us more
of what God is like. That
person's name was Jesus.

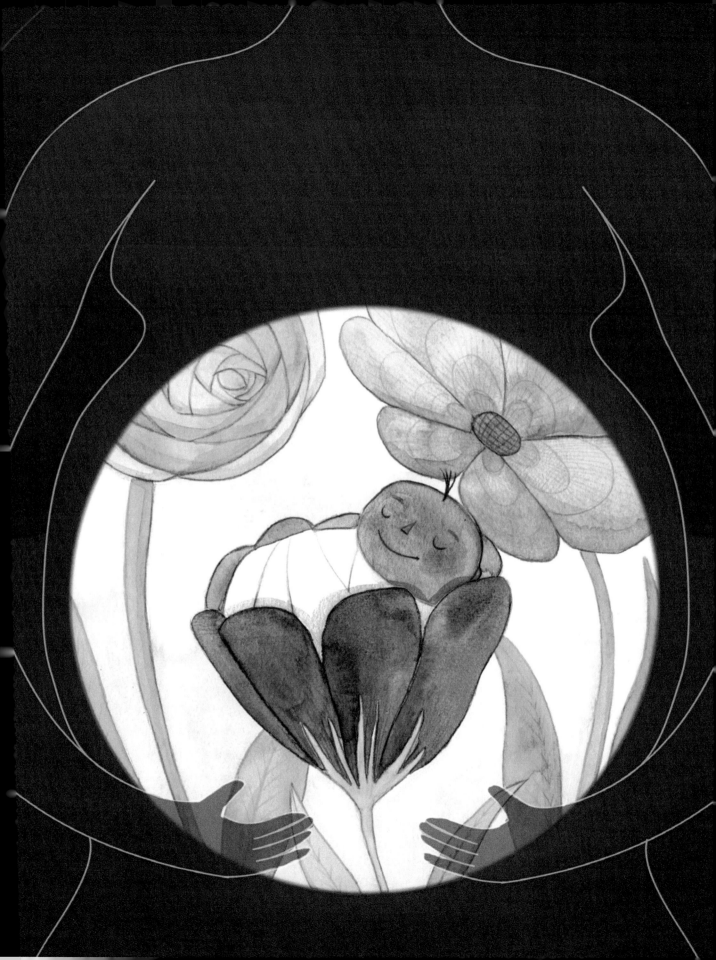

Jesus grew into a man and
showed us more of what
God is like.

He used his power to help
people who were sick.
This showed them that God
wants to help and care for
us no matter who we are.

Caring, wouldn't you say?

Jesus was so nice that he included everyone.

From mean bullies who took people's money to people who nobody wanted to be friends with, he hung out with everyone.

God is friends with everyone and doesn't reject anyone. That's very nice, don't you think?

Jesus showed everyone
how to love people who
are different from them.

Well, some people didn't
like how big and generous
Jesus' love was.

They were afraid of people
who were different from
them and wanted everyone
to be the same as them.

But Jesus accepted people
just as they were and was
showing everyone more of
what God was really like.

That's right. God is more
than nice - God is love
itself!

So, the people arrested
Jesus so they could
destroy him.

But Jesus didn't fight back
or hate them. No, he did
the opposite! Instead, he
forgave them.

God always forgives
everyone!

But soon after everyone thought that Jesus had been destroyed forever, people saw him walking around, alive and well!

He didn't want to fight back or get revenge. Jesus just wanted everyone to get along and to know that he loved them - no matter what.

Jesus showed that God's love cannot be destroyed!

Once, someone saw
Jesus in a garden.

She didn't recognize
that it was him at first
because he looked like
a gardener.   But when
he said her name, she
realized it was Jesus!

Others saw him walking on the
road and began talking with him.

But it wasn't until they stopped to eat dinner together with him that they finally realized it was Jesus!

Other people saw Jesus appear out of nowhere in their house.

They realized that God was with them when they felt afraid and alone.

When we look at Jesus, we see a picture of what God is like.

So, is God nice? Yes, but not in the way we might have expected! Even when it isn't easy, God always loves, forgives and includes everyone. This love is so full of life that it won't ever die! Nothing can stop it.

It's the way of true life.

God's love is inside all of us and we can share it with the whole world!

Can you spot Jesus working in the garden?

Can you see God's love in everyone working together?

We can even see God's love
blooming around us in
nature. God's love is
everywhere if you look for it.

Can you find Jesus' face?

You might be surprised
where you find God's love.

Keep looking...

What do you like most about God?

What is most confusing about God?

What is most scary about loving people like God loves people?

Where have you seen God's love around you?

What friend or family member can you talk with about these ideas? All these questions are tricky, but it's much easier if we ask them together!

Resources

If you or your child want to take compassionate action but don't know where to start, here are two organizations that are doing great work around the world. Check them out!

Alongsiders International
alongsiders.org

Preemptive Love Coalition
preemptivelove.org

Contact Author
evokepeace.com
davidtnagai@gmail.com

About the Creators

David Nagai is an artist and educator. His background is in community development, which led him to live and work in the slums of India for five years. He currently lives in Yokohama, Japan with his wife, Chami.

Victoria Adhikari is a freelance artist who studied fine arts at the Rhode Island School of Design. She currently lives with her husband, Hoi and her son in Los Angeles.

56662310R00038

Made in the USA
San Bernardino, CA
13 November 2017